Pundemonium Vol 2

James E. Larson

Lefse Press—Agoura Hills, Ca
ISBN: 979-8-9874392-2-7
eBook ISBN: 979-8-9874392-3-4
Title: *Pundemonium Vol. 2*
Author: James E. Larson
Digital distribution | 2022
Paperback | 2022

Dedication

The author dedicates this book to his loving family, wife Cindy, daughter Erica, and son Greg. They have had to listen to the author over the years trying out the various puns on them. They deserve recognition for enduring that pun-ishment.

Chapter One

Did you hear about the professional contortionist who had to bend over backwards in order to work at the circus?

Kate and Edith were an old time singing act. One day, they came to a decision that they would split up and start singing by themselves. A record producer wanted to record them one last time but they refused. The record producer learned the lesson that he could not have his Kate and Edith too.

Years ago, a swim suit manufacturer named Horace, was designing a swim suit that also acted as a life preserver. The press heard about this and invited him to a local pool to test the swim suit. The concept worked very well. A reporter came up with the headline in the next day's paper, "You can lead a Horace to water but you can't make him sink."

An old optometrist and his partner of many years decided to part. It seems they were always arguing and they never saw eye to eye.

There once was a woman electrician who was also a seamstress. She finally figured out an office slogan that worked for both businesses...it was, "Let me repair your shorts!"

Thor, the Norwegian God of Thunder, had a day off after fighting and defending all the other gods from harm. Somebody asked him does he feel pain from all his injuries....

He said, "I am Thor all over."

A dentist thought it was a good idea to rent some extra office space he had to a manicurist. Alas, the manicurist was always complaining about something to the dentist. It seems they were always fighting tooth and nail.

In France, where the famous tower in Paris was constructed, everyday all Parisians get an Eiffel.

A Shriner went to pick up a special hat he ordered. When he got there, he discovered they had made the hat three times as tall as he wanted. He wore it anyway but it made him sad. A fellow Shriner said to him, "Why such a long Fez?"

In Germany, home of the Autobaun, there is a little amusement park that has a ride with cars shaped like rolled small pastry with white frosting on top...the ride is called the Cinnabon.

Chapter Two

A movie studio hired an elephant trainer and his elephant for a movie. The trainer got paid well but the elephant had to work for peanuts.

A pet detective found a large group of missing lions...he had a lot of pride in how that case turned out.

There was a pirate years ago who did not raid ships for gold or jewelry...he only wanted their melons and cucumbers. He was known around the Caribbean Sea as the "Squashbuckler!"

In the Animal Kingdom, a Flamingo could argue that they think they are very smart. However, in reality, sometimes they don't have a leg to stand on....

A farmer in Ohio collected old wooden type harnesses that were usually used on oxen.
He was working on one example while he slipped and got his head stuck in the thing.
He was upset but he eventually laughed it off but still the yoke was on him.

Jack Benny, the old time comedian, always said even though he was way past 39 years of age, his age was 39...so you could say that counting past 39 was not his forte.

A certain actor was very good in the silent films, but that goes without saying....

A proctologist was very worried about his office surviving because he owed his suppliers a lot of money. His wife said not to worry, because he was always in arrears...

A guy was trying to decide which career path he should take...a barber or a proctologist. He flipped a coin...heads or tails.

A TV weather man in a small town in Colorado told his viewers that the next day's weather would be sunny and warm. The next day came and it was windy and it snowed a foot of snow. Let's just say he was not welcomed back at the TV station if you catch my drift....

A podiatrist I know has a great reputation of treating a certain particular foot problem...he is known as the arch-enemy of flat feet.

Two old men, who just moved into a strict retirement home, were playing on an old board game for a dollar a game. Somebody turned them in because the home had a no gambling policy. The police took them to the station because the two old men had a "checkered past."

Chapter Three

In old England there was a rather large fellow who had the reputation of being the finest dressed person around. The house he was living in, unfortunately, had a very, very small closet. One day, while in the closet dressing for a tea with the Queen, he proceeded to bend over and got his ascot.

A dentist, who was also a veterinarian, while working in his lab, came up with a breath mint for cows with bad breath. When a local farmer heard about this, he said, "I cud not believe it!"

A rancher in Texas, who only raised rabbits, was trying to teach a quartet of rabbits to sing. It did not work out well because one was always a hare off.

The sergeant in the Army loved the military so much... even so, he said his feelings were strictly platoonic.

One of a sheepherders favorite female sheep passed away suddenly...the sheepherder went right away to write up the ewelogy.

I heard there is an old man in Turkey that can predict the future only when he blows his nose. He is known around those parts as Nostrildamus.

There are some first time mothers with babies that think they know it all about when to stop nursing their babies. You could say that attitude was overweening.

An architectural student in Iowa who was taking a test to allow him to design an ear corn storage building, relied on his crib notes.

Electric cars always keep plugging along....

The stadium announcer during a Woman's Professional Football game was unsure if he should use the quarterback's married name or her maiden...he decided to use her married name. When the quarterback heard her married name on the speaker, she thought of a way to let the announcer which name she preferred, so she took a nee at the end of the first play.

A company is selling a home kit where you can put on your teeth wire retainers to correct your teeth.....it is called "Brace Yourself!"

Did you know when a writer gets a severe cramp in their hand when they are writing so much it is called having "Author-ites."

Chapter Four

You have all heard the story about Jonah and the large ocean mammal, right? Well, Jonah did actually have a whale of a time, but the whale eventually got rid of Jonah on the beach because the whale could not stomach him anymore.

The aircraft designer was testing his aircraft he designed to see if it was stealthy. Alas it was not as it was plane to see.

A sign on the wall of an orthodontist's patient's waiting room said, "Let us help you put your money where your mouth is!"

A shepherd in Iraq decided to make some clothes for sale from the wool he sheared off his sheep. However, his prices were extremely high compared to the other shepherds. The authorities thought so also and they had him arrested for fleecing his customers.

A massage shop operator had to close his doors because his employees always seemed to rub his customers the wrong way.

A barber in New York had such very high prices that everybody agreed that they all thought he was running a typical clip joint.

Midway through writing the book, "The Complete Guide to Repairing Socks and Things," the author quit. He said he was tired of the whole darn thing.

The workers at a fence factory, where they only made one kind of fence, decided to go on strike. Their storage yard location was already full of pickets.

At the "Smuckers Condiment" factory, a door where they add the ingredients to the mixes would not open. It was jammed.

A pet detective was asked if he wanted to work on a case that involved a male goose. He said he would take a gander at it.

Years ago, an adventurer named Juan took a river cruise exploring a little known river in Alabama. He took photos of himself and only a certain kind of river mammal. A magazine executive heard about the trip and ordered some photos. He ordered six of Juan and half a dozen of the otter.

Did you hear about the local marijuana dispensary that lowered his prices so low because he wanted to weed out the competition?

Chapter Five

One reason a new play on Broadway was called a turkey by the critics was because the cast was being paid such a poultry sum.

In Kansas City, a father who had a butcher shop known for its very tender meat, also had a son there shining shoes in the lobby. The father was just making filet while the son shines....

An old bell ringer in a church in Norway, got caught in the rope one day and tolled himself off.

The upholstery guy was working very long hours to finish a chair to meet a deadline. Luckily for the client, he tufted it out.

The doorbell installer was always annoyed with his boss. At the job site when the installer was discussing the doorbell features with the client, his boss always wanted to chime in.

The animal trainer was studying a book to learn more about his job during his job in the cage. One day, one of the animals attacked him while he was doing his studying and he was sent to the hospital.
    "What happened?" said a passerby.
    The trainer's friend said, "He was just reading between the lions."

Did you know all violinist play by ear?

A young cardiologist was trying to make a career choice. Should he go in the army and serve in a field hospital in the Middle East, or go on the staff of the Kettering Hospital in New York. He was caught between Iraq and a heart place.

In Mexico City, they built a large building with a dance floor on big springs to absorb any tremors from an earthquake. The first function was the Governors Ball and wouldn't you know it an earthquake hit the building during all the dancing. A reporter at the party put the headline in the paper next day, "That's the way the ball bounces."

A home inspector was walking through a home for a client who wanted to move in quickly. The inspector noticed the dining room floor had a dip in it and it needed some new supporting wood members underneath the floor. He told the client and a carpenter fixed it right away, joist in time.

A man in Riverside, California, does funerals services for pets and they are done in a movie theme. His service for rabbits is called, "From Hare to Eternity."

Chapter Six

The big angry bull on a farm just consumed many rectangular bundles of hay. He then scared everyone around him by giving everyone such a baleful look.

The kitchen helper's first job was to use a kitchen implement to separate the seeds from the pulp in tomatoes. The chef kept demanding that the helper go faster and faster. So in the end, the helper was just straining to keep up.

A grocery store owner wanted his son to set up a booth in the store to sell a large shipment of chickpeas that the owner ordered too much of by mistake. He also wanted his son at the booth to really talk up and praise the chickpeas, and also keep it a secret that he was the owner's son. His son did not want to do any of those things, in other words, he just did not want to spiel the beans.

An old musical instrument collector, who was overweight, had an odd habit of sometimes dressing up in a costume representing one of his old instruments and then going to parties. He also had a reputation of not telling the truth. At one party, he came dressed as an old harp like instrument he loved. Those people at the party that knew him said that it was appropriate that he came as a big fat lyre.

Among his many talents, a nuclear physicist liked to play with atoms. He would heat them up in a big fire in an attempt to change their charges from negative to positive. You could say he liked to have lots of ions in the fire.

Trying to be innovative, a banana plantation in South America tried to manufacture dresses out of the dried fibers of the banana skins. But alas, it did not work out to well as the dresses seemed to always bunch up in all the wrong places.

A long time ago, a young prince wanted to be a king right away. The authorities in the country said no, but they did give him a reign check.

An antique book buyer went to a old book store in London to buy a book that they advertised. The book store said it was a first edition of "A Christmas Carol." The buyer bought the book and took it to a book authenticator expert. The expert explained that the only way to authenticate a book is to compare it to a known original book. Alas when he did this, he discovered the book was a fake. The book buyer learned a hard lesson which was "Don't count your Dickens before they are matched."

An ear, nose, and throat doctor, who was known for being very expensive, built a new office building with some whimsical features. One of them was a cubical that had a large proboscis that you passed your payments through. Most patients thought this was very fitting as they felt they have been paying through the nose for years.

Chapter Seven

In Hollywood, the action figure "Rubberman" wanted to do a comedy movie. His agent said that was not feasible by any stretch of the imagination.

In England, an employee of a farm supply company, was told by his boss to design a luxury pig pen no matter the cost. "Just remember," said the boss, "the sty is the limit!"

There is a farmer in Iowa named Ole that rents out overnight stalls to farmers for their cows when they travel from a long distance. Ole also serves the cows food. Ole calls it the first cow "Rumen House."

In my research, recently I heard that William Shakespeare might have been prohibited from writing poetry for a short period during his lifetime. It seems he was bard for a couple of years as decreed by the city of Avon, England.

A west coast developer was building a new marina next to the Pacific Ocean. He said he had harboured that idea for a long time.

A customer at a pet shop bought a large turtle when the sales clerk said, "Why don't you buy another one?"
    "No," said the customer, "I have shelled out enough money on turtles already."

A man, who was somewhat drunk, went to rob a bank. In his stupor, he went into a musical stringed instrument store next door. Well he robbed that store. He figured he was still getting away with some kind of lute....

I heard in England an eccentric home builder constructed a new two bedroom home that has 10 toilets in it. Talk about "Loo-nacy!"

In the state of Idaho, where potatoes are king, a man who has a business that picks up people and drives them to where they want to go. As a gimmick, he dresses up in a costume that looks like a potato. He calls his business "Tuber."

Somebody wrote a book about flapjacks. I heard the book is selling like hot cakes....

I see where the world's biggest dump truck, which is bigger than a house, just got selected for the "Haul of Fame."

Chapter Eight

The owner of a Navy Surplus store was arrested the other day. He was selling U.S. Government bedding equipment that were supplied to him by thieves. However, the store owner was the only one who got cot.

It is fitting that the new head of the American Plumbing Association, who is a woman, wore pumps to her first meeting.

The founder of a large ketchup manufacturing company said he never thought his company would be the world's largest. He said that in "Heinz-site."

Did you know that certain parts of the modern toilet were invented by a gentleman named Mr. Crapper? He ultimately became very flushed with success.

The young medical students were studying to name all the bones that make up a human hand. The students were not taking the studying seriously thought the professor.
So he told them to knuckle down.

Two soldiers, John and Tom, who really did not like each other, challenged each other to see who could stand at attention in the hot sun without falling down. The first to fall was John, After John's recovery, Tom told John he fell down with grace. Tom was damning John with faint praise.

In a marina in London, a boat festival was taking place. All the boats were small and were pointed at both ends. Some of the boat owners were upset about how crowded the marina was, but generally everybody else thought the festival was all hunky-dory.

In a crowded dark room, a photographer's assistant was running some photos in a developing solution and was also eating his lunch's dessert to save some time. He accidentally knocked a developing photo into his dessert. All the people in that dark room agreed that this is what happened as the proof was in the pudding.

In ancient Rome, the weather one day turned nasty. Little round ice balls started to drop from the sky.
    "What are those little balls of ice called?" asked Caesar.
    A servant said, "Hail Caesar."
    Caesar said to the servant, "Thanks for the greeting, but just answer the question!"

A student, who was attending a contractor class on how to be an electrician, wired an electrical panel all wrong. He got angry and then blew a fuse.

A long, long time ago along the coast of South America, the natives made what we call today a surf board out of old roofing materials. Hence the origin of the old surfer expression, "Hang Tin!"

Chapter Nine

Ashepherd was having a very hard time to find one of his lost lambs. It seems the lamb definitely did want to be found as it had run away many times before. Alas the shepherd finally found the lamb out in the desert landscape. He was bleating around the bush.

A bee keeper in Kansas was formally charged the other day. He was running a honey making business without a permit. When he heard this, he skipped town. The local sheriff said, "He can run but he cannot hive!"

In Alabama, the owner of a plant greenhouse was known as someone very generous with her flowers, especially her favorite Peonis. When a customer came up to her without saying a word, the owner handed her a flower and said, "A peonis for your thoughts."

An architect went to a lumber yard and asked for a 2 x 4. The clerk asked him how long did he want it. The architect said he wanted it for a very long time as he was going to use it in a house he was building.

A husband wanted to surprise his wife on her birthday with a new sofa. He had the furniture store deliver it while she was at work. He wanted the sofa to be couched in secrecy.

Somebody did something wrong to a phlebotomist and now he is vengeful and seems to be just out for blood.

In Colorado, a carpentry shop sponsored a marathon race. One of the runners got lost and ended up running through a wheat field. He could not run very well as he kept going against the grain.

The owner of a shop for fisherman was arrested the other day. He was selling worms for fishing and also giving his employees corporal punishment with a branch from a hickory tree if they did not sell enough worms. The arresting cop said it was a classic case of "Bait and Switch."

I heard in new law in Scotland concerns the people who wear the tartan clothes skirt like apparel around their waist. You cannot wear it sloping down on one side. You can be fined if your apparel if "off-kilter."

A farmer in New England built a tree house up 50' high with steps nailed into the trunk.
   Somebody asked him if it was difficult to climb those steps and what kind of tree is it.
   He said it was a Beech to both questions.

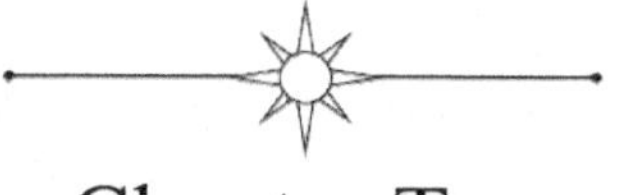

Chapter Ten

A window factory owner was told by a consultant that he should expand his business to maybe making full length mirrors. The factory owner said he would take the time to look into it.

A candle shop owner, who was very verbose, would often sing the praises of his candles.
He would often wax poetically about them.

A not so successful butcher, who specialized in just chickens, was always just trying to make hens meat.

Two monks became very good friends because of a chants meeting.

A shoe salesman at a shoe store fell in love with a shoe saleswoman. They became solemates.

A ballerina in Paris and her young daughter, after seeing a Can Can show, packed a tutu, which the daughter thought was too froo froo, flew to Pago Pago. After landing, her daughter fell and got a boo boo. The she ate something bad and got an ache in her tum tum. They took a choo choo down to the dock to board a ship to New York, New York. The ballerina said bye bye to the train conductor. When she boarded the ship, she asked the captain if there will be calm seas.

He said, "Aye aye."

On the ship, the ballerina danced the Cha Cha and ate Bon Bons. She said hello to the go go dancer and went ha ha with her jokes. When the ballerina was asked if she would like to be that kind of dancer, she went pooh pooh. When she boarded the plane to Paris, she found out that the in flight movie was "Boeing Boeing." Of course that was the movie, a movie in my opinion that never got off the ground.

A farmer in Missouri opened up a motel for pigs that travel with their owners. The motel has been quite successful. Of course when the motel is full, the owner lights up the sign down by the highway that says, "No Baconcy."

There was a guy, who loved old movie musicals, who made pottery for flowers, but also you could fill the pottery with water, blow over the top of them and create music. He also did auto body work on cars. He had a sign over his shop that said, "Lets vase the music and dents."

A fishing boat captain in Rhode Island announced to the press that he was going fishing tonight just for the Halibut.

Chapter Eleven

There is a large clothing factory in China that specializes in making clothes for monks.

The item they make is the hooded part of their outfits. Well, a recent shipment from the factory was stolen but then recovered by the police. The owner of the factory believes the police will take their time in returning the items. The police argue they will speed up the process. The owner and the police will probably be arguing about this until the cowls come home.

In London, a man robbed a bank and instead of escaping in a car, he escaped in a helicopter. He was going to fly to his very large tree less and shrub less land that was out of town. When he got there, he lightly touched down but then flew off when he saw the police waiting for him to land. Local people said he escaped by the skim of his heath.

A local restaurant had a promotion where they said anybody that can eat a 60 oz. steak in one siting, the meal would be free. Two good friends, Tom and John, stopped by. Tom kept pressuring John to enter the challenge and John kept trying to avoid it. So John eventually gave in and started to eat and over halfway through, he quit. John realized he had bitten off more than he could eschew.

Did you hear about a new store that only sells penne pasta and pound cakes? The customers who stop by always say, "In for a penne, In for a pound!"

In India, there are a group of people who carefully watch over the customs that the Indian people use when conducting their funerals and helping them if things get out of hand. That group of people is called the local Pyre Department.

It is a little know fact that when the telegraph company first started out, they did not pay their workers very much so in the northeastern United States in winter, many operators went without heat. So when the operators got sick and their noses got stuffed up, they said to their friends and their friends thought they heard them say they had a Morse Code.

A farmer in Africa had a problem with a herd of Wildebeests eating his crops. So he hired an expert to stop this from happening. Well, it worked. As the farmer said, "No Gnus is good Gnus!"

In the 1980's, a man who was a very new dog owner, had a haircut that was short on the top and sides but very long on the back. Well, the new dog must have thought that much hair was the owner's tail. Finally, after trying to resist doing so, the dog felt he had no choice but to just bite the mullet.

Chapter Twelve

In old Italy, a new hire in a sawmill was assigned the job of taking the outer rough layer off certain trees before they are sent into the mill. One day he made a mistake and took the outer rough layer off the wrong tree. His supervisor yelled at him and said, "Tony, how many a times do I gotta tell ya, you are debarking up the wrong tree!"

In Paris, a man was on trial for robbing a bank that happened to be next to the grand main river that runs through Paris. His lawyer was hoping to use an insanity defense. He said his client, who had jumped into that river after the robbery, was literally in Seine at that point.

A skilled wood carver made a trumpet instrument out of wood. When he played it, it sounded good but he had a lot of trouble controlling the pitch.

A bee keeper who supplied honey to the Transcontinential Railroad workers a long time ago, was credited with the words for a popular song. Does anybody remember the song, "Hive Been Working on the Railroad."

A group of environmentalists went to a metal fabrication shop to have the shop build them an item they wanted. The group wanted a very large rake they could pull behind a truck on a beach in order to collect trash. Later, a film documentarian company, after seeing the group collecting trash on the beach, wanted to tell their story. The owner of the film company, who was a big baseball fan, titled the film, "If you build it they will comb."

Many years ago, there was a phenomenon concerning the selling of an item called a "Pet Rock" which consisted of a small rock in a box with instructions on how to care for it. I had heard the "Pet Rock" was kind of shy, but now I expect it is more boulder now.

In Denver, a beautician who works on large animals, had a client that had a large male deer. The beautician was combing the hair down on the forehead of the deer when she asked the client, "How does that look?"

The client told her she needs to make that hair look bigger on the deer's forehead.

"After all," said the client, "I want more bang for my buck!"

Almost everyone know about the story of William Tell shooting an apple off the head of his son. Later in life I heard he wrote a book about his life and some of the mistakes he admitted to in life. The title of the book was "I saw the arrow of my ways."

Chapter Thirteen

A surgeon, who specializes in appendectomies, wrote a book about his many operations over his very long career. However, his book publisher told the doctor that the book would be too thick and he would need to make the book a little thinner. The surgeon agreed and like he had done many times before, he quickly removed the appendix.

The owner of a door manufacturing company was on trial for selling a defective door that was not strong enough to prevent a home robbery. The lawyer for the owner was told by the company owner that whatever the lawyer does, the lawyer does not talk bad about the door until after the trial. In other words, the lawyer was told, "Don't knock it till you try it!"

A person owned a hat shop next to a marina. A man ran into the shop right after his small boat sank and he was trying to find somebody to help. Before he could ask, the shop owner said, "Capsize?"

The boat owner said, "How did you know already, it just happened!"

A tree nursery owner was fined the other day. He was caught selling tropical trees as drought tolerant trees to naive customers. The fine was for trying to palm off the wrong trees to people.

In a southern state in the backwoods of that state, a naive, ignorant, foolish person decided he wanted to get into politics. He is now running as the goobernatorial candidate for governor.

At a river's edge in the old west, two inept men were trying to tie logs together to make something that would float them down the river. Their incompetence at binding a bunch of logs together was the source of a raft of jokes by the nearby spectators.

In England, a retired boxer went into a new business where he only provides the filling for pillows for clients who are royalty. His office motto is, "I am down for the Count!"

In China, a class on cooking etiquette was being conducted. The instructor discussed how chefs and their helpers should talk with each other and also how they should correctly handle their utensils. She said when the chefs argue with a helper, the helper should always know how to hold their tong.

A shoemaker in China discovered how to make soles of shoes that mimic the soft padding of a mole which is a small animal. With his expected profits, he wants to build a small village and dedicate it to the former Chairman Mao. You could say he wanted to make a Mao Town out of a mole heel.

Chapter Fourteen

id you know the first candle maker made such a fuss over the fact that the buyer of the candle had the choice of deciding which end to light? He was just burnishing the candle at both ends.

A manicurist was working on a customer when her chair just collapsed and as she was falling, one of the customers fingers hit the manicurist on the forehead.

"Bad chair," said the customer.

"You just hit the nail on the head," said the manicurist.

An old time roofer was working on a house. He had a tradition where he would wash the first shingle before he would install it on the roof. He said he always wanted to just start every job with a clean slate.

A fisherman brought his catch into a shop near the dock. The shop had refrigerators that people could store their fish and keep them fresh. Even though there was a line at the counter and he was kind of upset about the wait time, he remembered that another fisherman told him this store was the place to cool his eels.

A cowboy rode up to the hitching rail and was about to tie up his horse when he noted there was a large hornets nest on a branch of a tree by his head. He quickly undid the things on the saddle that you put your feet through to ride and immediately threw them at the nest. The cowboy's friend said, "That certainly one way to stirrup a hornets nest!"

A bill collector from a bank was making demands on a man who insisted that he did not owe any money. The man called the bank manager, who was a woman, to say there must be some mistake. Sure enough, the manager said a mistake had been made. Just like the old movie title, "She Dun Him Wrong."

A hair dresser went on a picnic early one morning and she decided to roll on the wet grass and her hair got all messed up. She discovered that when it comes to her hair, it takes dew to tangle.

At Honolulu airport there is a company that tries to greet all people when they depart the arriving plane. Once in a while, the company arrives late but they do show up eventually. The company's motto is, "Better lei-ed then never."

About the Author

The author, James E. Larson, has always enjoyed a good pun. Just recently, he decided to create new ones for a book. He says like anything else, some puns come easy while other need some rewrites before they are finished. A good pun needs a good back story that sets up the 'Pun-ch Line.' That is the fun part of creating puns.

www.ingramcontent.com/pod-product-compliance
Lightning Source LLC
Chambersburg PA
CBHW020656160726
47991CB00003B/1210